Hello, my name is Corey Nelson, let me start by saying; life is a roller-coaster that never ends. Filled with a ton of up's and down's, twists and turns. Life is very unpredictable. So, if you think life is intended to be easy and everything's a handout, your wrong. I wrote this book because I have a unique story to tell about my life. However, we all may have a good story to tell. When you read mine, you will see the highs and lows of life, the challenges, and the battles I've fought to get to who I am today.

My goal is for this book to be an inspiration and a voice for those that need it. Life will never be easy and will not be as you have envisioned it, but it's led by you. Each situation and how you handle it helps make or breaks your path. Your path in this life is up to only you to make it the best it can be.

Your past doesn't define your future, I'm proof of that. Nobody, I don't care who has the right to tell you, you can't do something. A lot of people in life told me I couldn't do a lot and I almost believed it, don't.

This book is an extended version of Chapters of Life published in December 2018; you will see quite a few similarities, being that most of the story is the same. However, the difference in this book is more detail. About 10 more pages of content were added, plus my life since publication.

Please be advised: the first chapter can be overwhelmingly depressing, upsetting, and possibly disturbing to some. What you are about to read is very raw; nothing is held back. I wrote this book as best as I can remember, in no way is this a form of bashing

people. **This book includes; adult language, content,**

and situations, reader discretion advised.

About the book

This book is an autobiography about how challenging life can be, it can inspire a lot of people that have faced a lot of adversity through life. I grew up in foster care since the age of three; I also was born with a physical disability. This book is about someone who was born with a disability and has had to overcome a lot of challenges. He knows what it's like to feel the lowest of lows and the highest of highs. Life is hell at times but it's always going to improve.

This book goes in chronological order about the first thirty years of my life. Each chapter is about on either a set of years or life event. I discuss everything, how I felt, and things I had to do to move forward. If any of my exes read this and don't like it, well, I don't care, just like you didn't give a crap about hurting me. Thanks for giving me a story and making me rich.

This guy with a disability called Cerebral Palsy has done and experienced more than anyone would think without having a chance to talk to him. Some of the experiences are good. However, others are the worst of the worst. With that, I hope you enjoy reading this book! This is **an extended version** of Chapters of Life released in December 2018.

Chapters

In some chapters I talk about my travels to give advice. In this book there will be a section in the back providing more advice.

Chapter One:

I Didn't Ask for This...

I was born on September 4th, 1988, with Cerebral Palsy (CP), in Connecticut. I didn't live in Connecticut for long, so I do not remember anything about living in Connecticut. I think I've been living in Florida ever since before I was two years old. I know nothing about my family background or anything of that nature, throughout the reading you will find out why.

I was born with CP, the umbilical cord was wrapped around my neck, so I was born not breathing.

Cerebral palsy known as "CP" is a motor system disorder that has different effects on different individuals. CP does not, again I repeat DOES NOT affect mentality. Some like myself, have full functionality of their limbs. However, some may not. CP for me affects my speech and movement. When I walk, I have a limp; also, at times when I communicate, I'm misunderstood by some. When I'm too excited or stressed out, two things are likely to happen, involuntarily; spazzing movements and yelling or un-understandable speech.

I sometimes raise my voice like I'm angry and don't know I'm doing so. Because of that, and the motions, I can come off very mad even when I'm not. I get very irritated and embarrassed because of that.

Also, with my CP, sudden loud noises will make me jump, even if I know it's coming, another embarrassing thing, can I control it? No, I wish I could. And maybe if more people understood it, I wouldn't have gone through some of the things I have. I have a type of CP called "Spastic CP."

In most cases, CP happens due to lack of oxygen to the brain, near or during birth, as it did for me, the more time without oxygen the more severe the effects can be. There is no known cure for CP as of now. It is not hereditary, meaning if I had kids, me having CP, wouldn't play a fact in them having it or not. Also, CP can't get worse, if you take care of yourself and know your limits, but it has its peak. In fact, for some, it can get better.

The first five years of my life I used a wheelchair and walker. Walking was very difficult for me as a young boy, especially for long periods of time. I wore a helmet until I was ten because I would fall all the time. I also wore leg braces every day to make me walk as best as possible. As I was growing, I got stronger, with the help of therapy.

I have a brother, and he was born on August 28th, 1990. So, we are exactly a year, eleven months and three weeks apart. When I was three years old, my brother and I went into foster care because of severe physical and mental abuse, by both our mother and father. When we got placed into foster care, we moved to a foster home in Palm Harbor, FL. We were welcomed as a part of their family right away.

The family we lived with was great. My foster dad was a sheriff officer. Which I thought was cool and made me want to be one when I grew up until I got old enough to realize, because of my disability I wouldn't qualify. The mother stayed at home with us kids. A few years later we moved to a neighborhood called Countryside in Clearwater. Before we moved into that house, we spent a while looking at other houses, I remember being in the van going house hunting with them.

The house we got had five bedrooms and three baths. They did a lot of remodeling to the front and inside the house quickly after we moved in. the house also had a screened-in pool.

Our family had about ten people. 4 of their own who were older than us foster kids, and 3 or 4 foster kids at a time. My Brother and I were the longest foster kids they had in their home. They had a foster daughter they quickly adopted; I think even before we moved in. While we were in the foster home, our biological parents still had occasional supervised visitation with us.

Aside from staying with this family, we stayed with a few others and in one grope home. There's one group home I remember from this time period. The group home was called The Sally House and it was run by The Salvation Army. I liked the home ok, and the staff was nice. At the Sally House, I watched a lot of movies; Dumbo was one of them, I think I watched it every day and soon became my favorite.

When I was six years old, my brother and I went back to our biological parents. However, they didn't learn their lesson and they did the same thing. So, after a year, we got removed by DCF again when I was seven, and we moved back to the same family we were with before. I believe this time we were taken away because school employees called the police after seeing a lot of bruises on me.

I remember going to Tyrone Elementary in St. Petersburg for a short time, as I was staying with my biological parents. I liked Tyrone, and this school did something different. To get on and off the bus at school the bus backed into a dock and we went through the back-exit door.

A few months after being taken away for the second time, my biological parent's parental rights got revoked. Not allowing anymore contact between my parent's and myself until I was eighteen. The last time I saw my parents, I was seven, we were in the courthouse. My parents are walking out of the courtroom as I was being escorted in by my DCF worker to testify against my parents, but I guess the case was called early and before I entered courtroom the judge had already made a ruling, and the ruling was; all parental right terminated. At that moment I really didn't know how to feel, but I remember seeing them in passing, and I did cry, I'm not sure why. About a week before the hearing I was in an empty courtroom to practice my testimony. I didn't know how to feel during the practice; I think to talk about it made me feel ashamed. I believe I was selected because I was the oldest out of my brother and myself.

I went through years of counseling because of what happened to me. I think the counseling started after the second time I was put back in foster care. At first, I didn't even like discussing what had happened; I felt ashamed, and like I was to blame, as most foster kids do. As sessions continued, I felt more comfortable talking, and the talking helped. I saw that I was not to blame, I was the victim. If my younger brother was in counseling too, I can't only imagine how he felt.

There are times even now as a 30-year-old man I remember what I had to go through and all the counseling. Let me point out that most foster kids feel the way I felt at first, and this feeling can cause mental issues. As you will see I had some mental issues as a teenager, but I outgrew them.

The abuse was harsh, and I believe that what I remember was from the one year when I was back with my parents at six years old. We got beaten with belts and paddles all the time. And I strongly believe most of the beatings were for no reason at all. Every night our father watched us sleep, if we opened our eyes, even slightly to blink, we'd get rubber bands shot at us. Most of the time his aim was good, and I got hit hard. Image laying down for bed and not being able to open your eyes for not even a second. I still to this day remember the trauma as I'm writing this book. I always get scared when someone points a rubber band at me as if they're going to shoot one at me. The only time we were safe from it was out in public. For instance; The only time I remember feeling safe was when we were on the city bus because they wouldn't hit us in front of people.

Aside from the daily abuse my father was a drunk pervert, he exposed himself in our backyard one night, he had us outside by our swing set in the middle of the night and dropped his pants. I believe he only did something like that once. I get asked; "Do you want to look for your parents?" I have always said. "No! Hell no!" and that will most likely never change. In my opinion they have no right even to know me.

If I ever ran into them, I wouldn't say a damn word. If I did it be, "Hey, fuck you and go to hell", honestly. I mean they are sick individuals that 1 didn't give a shit about my brother or myself. The man reason I feel this way is because they had a second chance, but they chose to fuck that up. For this reason, I believe if kids are taken away from there biological parents it should stay that way.

Around this time, I was in the second grade at Palm Harbor Elementary. And I began starting to lose focus. School became difficult, and I just became a big slacker; I didn't take the work, test, and grades seriously. Because of that, I failed the second grade and retook it. When I repeated the second grade, I was no longer in regular classes

From second grade on I was in Exceptional Student

Education known as ESE. I took my second and third

grade at Lilia G. Davis and had a strict teacher, I gave

her a lot of problems. The classwork was a joke to me,

and I liked being a "Class clown." I did my fourth and

fifth grade school years at one of my favorite schools,

Eisenhower.

While my brother and I lived together we were

inseparable; we did almost everything together. Most

times I followed his lead, even though I'm the older

brother. I think I followed his lead because he doesn't

have a disability. We also went to the same schools

together for about two years. Growing up my favorite

time of the year was October to December, because of

the fall weather and the holidays where everyone

came together a lot. I really enjoyed staying in this home and my brother and I were very close. I can say this was the best foster home I stayed at.

We had a big extended family and family friends, ant's uncle's, grandparents and more. During the holiday's our house was full of everyone, almost every year, for all holidays. I remember these gatherings every year, and it's one thing I have missed for a long time. For Halloween our yard was one of the best on the block, our front yard was a graveyard. And my dad had a friend, and both dressed up to pass out candy. I liked dressing up and going trick-or-treating, but that was something we kids only got to do if our behavior was good. Because of my behavior, especially after the age of eight, some years I didn't go.

For Christmas we had a lot of decorations too, as times I'd be outside watching stuff be put up. I watched dad I watch dad do a lot including when he worked out. I was close with dad; he nicked named me Cor-man after he did a lot of others followed suit. Especially some of our aunts and uncles.

Aside from relatives, my mom hung out with a friend and the friends' son became my best friend growing up. One time my friend and I went to a place called Celebration Station which had food and games inside plus go-carts and other rides outside. The go-carts were my favorite thing to do there, and something I did a lot whenever I went there. Celebration Station was my favorite place to go and I went there quite a few

times. Even when I got older, I got to go with other

families. We hung out a lot and I sometimes stayed the night. One night I was on the top bunk of bunk beds and I fell off, I then had to be rushed to the emergency room where I needed stitches.

My family made trips together too, and they were fun. Our excursions included Disney World and Busch Gardens, where we went a few times. I didn't ride that many rides because I didn't like to, and most of the roll-o-coasters look scary to me. However, there was a time where I was forced to try a few rides, which made me feel very uncomfortable. Some coasters I have yet to sill ride even today. The loops and being up-side-down a lot is something I hate. Some roll-o-coasters at Bush Gardens, Tampa Bay, have your feet dangle,

I hate that too. However, there were rides like Rino Rally I went on that I liked. I also liked bumper cars; Bush Gardens had that too. I remember going to the Zoo a few times too. One time they had what I remember to be a foster kid's day. They had a small town set up, and we kids got to go around this town like adults on our own. I thought this was cool and had a lot of fun.

Aside from going to theme parks, we went out to eat. Two of my favorite restaurants were Hops and Hooters, which is still my favorite, because of their wings. The Hooters we went to was the original location in Clearwater, FL. Root Beer was one of my favorite soft drinks as a young kid.

We also took road trips, to Georgia, at least four times, Tennessee- the Smoky Mountains, and Louisiana. We went to an Army base in Louisiana where their son was based. I enjoyed long road trips in the car. And still do. To me its 0fun seeing other parts of the country. When the went to Louisiana we drove to the Texas state border to take a picture of us standing in front of their welcome sign.

My brother and I soon found out how much Florida sucked, and we even sang it in the car; "Florida sucks, it really really sucks." I believe the main reason why we thought and still think Florida sucks is the climate. You know how they say Hell is hot? Well we say, Florida is Hell's waiting room. From the first time we felt weather out of Florida We've felt that way

Living in that family was great, and I still have flashbacks on memories to this day. We had a lot of toys, like; hot wheel cars and blocks to create things, we played a lot together. We also had video and computer games. We liked and watched a lot of cartoons together too. Some night on weekends us boys would stay up late in our room watching cartoons. I also liked little kids shows like Mr. Rodgers, Teletubbies, and sesame street. Also, as much as I'd hate to admit I liked Barny until almost the age of 11.

For outside activities we all had bikes. I, however, had a trike. I loved riding it as often as I could. One favorite childhood memory was watching the other kids play video games. My favorite types of video games were and still is racing games.

However, we had only one racing game and many more. Growing up we had Nintendo 64, PlayStation and our own Gameboy each. Watching people to me was more fun than playing, plus, some games I knew I couldn't successfully play. I still like watching others play but I also play now too.

The only thing I didn't like about staying with them was being forced to learn to swim. I know swimming is a good thing to learn but, swimming was always a challenge for me if I wasn't in the shallow water, I wasn't able to keep my head above water. I do understand that swimming was good exercise, but I didn't like it at all. We had a pool, and when the others wanted to go in, I had to join. The swimming pool wasn't a choice for me; I had to go in and when mom and dad got in they made sure I stayed away from the shallow end for a little bit. The pool, at times, was used as a punishment at times. One time I got into trouble at school so when I got home, they had me sit by the pool. So, when it would storm, which happens a lot in Florida, I liked it; because it's unsafe to be in a pool when it's storming outside.

By the age of about nine, my CP was improving a lot, I no longer needed the assistance of a wheelchair or walker. Surgery began being discussed as a good option for me when I was about ten years old.

At eleven years old, I had surgery done on both legs, to loosen my tendons in my knees and heel cords, to improve my walking. I was scared about the whole process of surgery at first. I thought to myself, "What if I wake up in the middle of surgery?" Immediately right after the surgery, I woke up, and I tried to get up to walk, but I couldn't. I had to stay in the hospital for a day and a half. The first-night mom and dad brought me some stuff; one was the Buzz Lightyear movie. Toy Story was one of my favorite movies and Buzz was my favorite character. So, my first night in the hospital I watched that.

Follow my release from the hospital I was in casts for six weeks, so for most of the time, I was stuck in a wheelchair. I also could not shower by myself, my foster mom had to help me most of the time. I believe I felt kind of embarrassed about this.

There were times the other kids and I were outside, and they were riding their bikes, I couldn't and didn't like that.

Being in a wheelchair most of the time sucked, I hated it and wished I could get out of it more than I was able to. Witched was funny because before I was in the wheelchair, I had wished I could use one more than I got too. At the end of the six weeks, the cast came off, and when they did, I had to learn to walk all over again which was a pain.

My legs were never able to bend, while in casts. So, when they came off, bending my legs was extremely painful, it felt like I broke bones in my legs every time I had to bend them. Due to the excruciating pain, I was in; we went back to the hospital a few days later. The doctors in the hospital knew what was wrong and a way to make it better, with that, I had to wear leg braces to bed every night for at least the next five years. If I didn't my legs stayed bent the entire night, making it very painful the next day. For weeks, after the surgery, I had Physical therapy at home and the hospital.

However, after all, the operation made a significant life improvement for me and I'm thankful for that. Before the surgery I use to sit with my legs bent beside me, it's called "W sitting" ever since the surgery, I haven't been able to sit like that. I also can't sit Indian style either.

Also, after surgery, I no longer needed braces during the day to walk or a helmet. They tried braces after surgery and saw the braces were making my walking worse and was potentially a safety concern. The braces I wore before my surgery just went to my knees, and the new ones they tried went up to almost my hip.

Meanwhile, in school, I was in speech therapy until the fourth grade, and I was in physical and occupational therapy until about the sixth grade. Most therapy sessions were every week and I got pulled out of class for about an hour. I completed the fifth grade there at Eisenhower, about four months before the end of school I asked my teacher to teach me multiplication, he did, and I was the only one in the class learning it. I progressed so well that he introduced division.

When we graduated, our fifth-grade graduation song was; "I Believe I Can Fly," which has been my go-to song for karaoke to this day. Still, after elementary school, I was in ESE. Most of the time I didn't like being in ESE classes and wanted to be in the regular education classes. Also, in school, I was one of those kids that would go off quickly if I was being made fun of, which happened a lot. I believe bullying contributed to some of my teenage behavior you will read about.

Around the age of 9 and 10, I also had a mentor who would take me out and spend a few hours a week with me. We went to parks, a mall, and other places. I liked going to car dealerships, and I'm not sure why. So, he took me to a few, and I liked looking at new cars and trucks. Speaking of cars, I can remember all the vehicles the family had; first was a red 16-passenger Ford Van. And one day we were riding when I saw a fire starting in the very back of the van, so I immediately said, not yelled, in a soft tone, "Fire" we all got out. We next had a green GMC 9-passenger van and then a white 3-row Ford Expedition.

When I was about eleven, I appeared on Wednesdays Child on 10 News here in Tampa Bay, FL; Wednesdays Child was a news segment about kids that were up for adoption. My caseworker took me, and the shooting of the interview was in a mall, and I believe close to the holiday season. I was being asked in the interview to say a bit about myself and what I wanted for Christmas; a big toy firetruck I saw in the toy store was what I really wanted. My current foster home at the time was still questioning adopting me because I started having behavior issues.

When I was about twelve, my behavior got worse; I was very defiant, calling 911 when it wasn't needed, destroying property, and running away constantly. I was a terrible influence and one time I encouraged my brother to run away with me. In group homes, I pulled the fire alarm.

I didn't care about anything or anyone but myself. I'm not sure why I had had all these problems suddenly. I did twelve hours in a boot camp with the sheriff's office, as an attempt to try and fix my behavior. However, it didn't work.

I was baker acted about 15 times in six months because of my behavior and running away. The first few times I was backer acted I was taken to Morton Plant Hospital; I was there so often I was confined to my room one time. I also went a few times to the crises center at PEMHS. A backer act is a three day stay in a hospital where you see a psychiatrist, attend groups, and see a therapist. My first few times being backer acted I acted out a lot, but then I calmed down because

I knew they were not going to tolerate it and there was no escaping.

I didn't like authority and thought I knew better. I wanted to do what I wanted when I wanted, no one could get through to me. I moved to about seven different foster homes and 3 group homes, in that same time span, from south Pinellas to north Pasco County. There are two homes I vividly remember.

The first was in Dunedin, and there were a lot of kids there, so much that we had an 18-passenger van. I stayed in this home three times, even before my behavior issues started.

We went to church and Kid's World, the first

time at Kid's World I hated it because it was so loud; I

also went to a hockey game. I liked this home ok, but I

do remember overhearing abuse. I stayed in this home

quite a few times and it was in Dunedin, Fl. The second

home was in New Port Richey. I was there for two

weeks and liked it ok. However, one day the parent

banged my head into a wall.

Some of the homes I liked ok, but a lot of them I

didn't. Some places I wasn't there for more than 30

minutes, if I didn't like one thing about the place I was

at, I'd do or say anything to leave, sometimes leaving

these homes led to being baker acted. I almost got

adopted by one family and stayed like two weeks with

them, but I decided to act up, so I wouldn't get adopted by them.

       I still had hopes of staying with my brother. Because my behavior was terrible, I never got adopted. Thinking I would be adopted by the family that had my brother was foolish after all the trouble I caused them. Also, in that same time span, the foster family I grew up with, with my brother, took me back eight times. So, I had chance after chance to stay with them and my brother and them, but I never changed, and at times have regretted it. As I have gotten older, I have regretted it less and less. As I'm writing this, I'm about 31 and my brother is 29, if I would of stayed, I wouldn't have written this or experienced a fraction of what you will read throughout this book. I talk to my brother on a regular basis, he still lives at home, no higher education, and no experiences like me, and it makes me sad for him as his older brother.

There were a few days where my caseworker had to spend all day trying to find me a placement. wen foster homes and group homes got background information on me, a lot of them didn't want me, due to my behavior. So, on those days, I stayed all day in the DCF office.

One time as I was in the office all day, I helped by running back and forth making copies and retrieving printouts for the staff. I liked doing it too and thought it was fun. For most years the DCF office, for my area, The Suncoast region, was in the "300 building" they called it, on 5th avenue and 34th street in St. Petersburg.

Due to my behavior, I started taking medications for ADHD and depression; I also started behavior health counseling sessions regularly. Counseling and drugs would be a part of my life for the next several years. At first, I was on a lot of medication and taking it two to three times a day, I also had medication just for sleeping, because I began having sleeping problems. The behavior counselor started coming out to the home when I was still with my brother, but for some reason, it didn't help, so, I couldn't stay there.

Chapter Two:

Teens

My brother and I got separated. He got adopted, I got kicked out. At the time, my brother got adopted I was living with them, I was even in the courtroom as the adoption happened. After being kicked out, I went to a mental health program for teens with behavior issues. It was a lockdown facility, but nothing like a detention center.

We had outings, and I got along well with

people there, including the staff. Most of the time we were outside playing in our courtyard or watching movies. The program had a point system, points were based upon your behavior and personal goals, depending upon your points you were on a level. The higher you level, the more you got to do; like go on outings and later bedtime.

When I entered the program, it had just started less than a month ago. The program was called CAP, run by Personal Enrichment through Mental Health Services, PEMHS. I was in some trouble there but not much, knowing I couldn't escape, made me not act up as much. I was in the program for four months then I moved to another foster home.

The new foster home was what they call a therapeutic foster home because the parents had more training for dealing with behavior issues and counselors came regularly. These types of foster homes were managed and operated within the collaboration of PEMHS. When I first moved in, I got a weekly allowance for doing chores, but I believe that stopped after the first year or so. I also remember for Christmas one year I got a new trike, which I liked. I went on bike rides every chance I got. One time I rode it 20 blocks from home and back, but that was years later.

We went to yearly summer camps; it was fun. The camp included all therapeutic foster kids and the PEMHS group home, it lasted 4 days, and was at camp

Florida in Brandon, an hour away. We had 24/7 staff in every area though. The camp had a talent show, I entered it for the first two years I went. I went to the camp about 4 times and I had fun, I fit in with the others which made me feel good.

The foster home was a single-parent home, aside from her role as a foster parent she had a full-time job. As far as I know, I was the longest foster child she had. I had one other foster brother there when I first moved in, after him I had another foster brother and two sisters after the second brother.

As I had a wheelchair one of my brothers and I stole a CD, from FYE at Tyrone Mall. He put the CD in my wheelchair, I sat down, and he pushed me out of the store. However, mom quickly found out and we returned it and banded from that store. After about another 6 months or so this brother left and another brother moved in. we got along for a while but one night after a few months this brother talked me into sex with him, I was 15 I agreed then right away I felt bad and sick. I hated myself for what I had done. The foster mom forced me to go to sex offender counseling because of it. I was very ashamed and felt like this was unnecessary. I felt bad right after the incident but now I had to go to this group and relive it. My foster mom didn't understand that I was talked into it by him.

After the foster brother moved out I had two sisters moved in. One of my foster sisters lived there with me for a long time of two years and I still have

contact with to this day. We talk regularly on the phone

and sometimes meet up. I was with this foster parent for

four years, until the age of seventeen. I went to middle

school for the seventh and eighth grade at Morgen

Fitzgerald in Pinellas Park. In 2004, two years after my

brother and I were living in different homes, my brother

and his adoptive family moved to Georgia.

After school, we had to go to after-school

programs. I went to RClub for a little bit at first, then

the Boys and Girls Club in Pinellas Park. Here there

was a separate center for teens; it was the first teen

center of its kind that opened. It was youth empowered

and almost different from the

rest of the boys & girls club. We teens decided outings, our budget, and other events. We had weekly meetings, elections for leaders, and voting. The two adult staff members we had was just there to oversee, they were very friendly and laid back. The teen center did outings together, dances, and more. Most outings and activities were after hours, like late nights or weekends, and if you planned on going, you had to sign up beforehand.

I was an active member of the teen center for about three years. I made some friends there, but the friendship was not outside there. A lot of these friends were 3 to 4 years older than me. When I first was there, we had a snack bar. I worked it for a bit, but they closed it down.

About a year after I moved into this new foster home, we moved from Pinellas Park to St. Petersburg. My mom works a job as an adult AIDS caseworker Monday through Friday. So sometimes when my mother would go to work, I would go to the library if I wasn't in school. One summer I began going to the library a lot. It was going to the library that got me interested in Web Design and Information Technology because at the library I was always on the computer.

They had a computer that people with disabilities could reserve for up to 3 hours at a time. So, sometimes I sat on a computer for 4 or more hours. I started teaching myself how to make a website and customizing homepages, and I also created my first social media account. My first social media account was on Myspace. Then maybe a year later I made a Facebook account.

I was also a volunteer in the library for a year and a half. My rolls as a volunteer were; assist people in checking out books by using, a self-checkout machine, stamping old books, organizing, and shelving books. When I became a volunteer, I rarely went on the computer at the library. I was a volunteer for a year and ten months.

The foster mother had friends that she hung out with regularly. Most of the meetups were at a bookstore at the mall. So, we were there at least every other week or more. As she hung out with her friends, I walked the mall. I think this led me to become, what they call a mall rat. One day in a store, a grown man that was standing beside me grabbed my junk.

I was terrified. He asked, "Want me to do it again?" I pretended not to understand, do what? I said. 2 minutes later, I know what you did, I said. He takes off running, and I try to follow. As I do, I get mall security. We are not able to find him, but store security cameras see him running, and then me running shortly after him. I was about fourteen when this happened.

I gain some independence, at fifteen I started riding city buses all over the county, my foster mom let me and even gave me money for the days. It was just

something I liked to do. But why? I bet some of you are

wondering. Well, it was the only good memory I had

from my biological parents. It was the only time I was

safe from the abuse. I also liked the freedom it gave me.

In 2004, I started ninth grade at Dixie M.

Hollins High in St. Petersburg, My first semester of

school I was in a class with much lower functioning

students than myself. It was a mistake, I didn't like it

and felt so out of place. It got fixed by the next

semester; I was in the right classes for me.

We had JROTC at my school; I knew because a

friend from the teen center was in it at this same school.

Which is why I wanted badly to go to this school. I investigated this program after a few weeks of school. After my determination, I was in JROTC in my second semester until I graduated.

I moved up ranks over the years, and for two years I was a supply room assistant. I enjoyed wearing the uniform, every Wednesday we wore class Bs to school.

I got to take part in after-school activities with JROTC; like being on honor guard. We dressed in BUD's on Fridays if there was a home football game. The honor guard, at home football games, fired a cannon, we used gunpowder.

The cannon went off at the start of the game, at halftime, and when we scored. The cannon took about a minute to reload, my role was firing it. For safety reasons they couldn't have me in the positions where we reload the cannon. Aside from being on honor guard, I traveled with my drill team to drill meets. I wasn't on the team because I wasn't able to do the drills, but I could be there to watch and support. I also participated in fundraising events and toys for tots with JROTC. I really enjoyed my time in JROTC and made quite a few friends.

In the actual JROTC class, I did well, I didn't do the drills because it was difficult, but I did most everything else. I was a supply room assistant for my class period.

I learned about first aid, marksmanship, and overall how to be a better person. During marksmanship, I got to fire an air rifle. The sergeant helped me, and the room was empty. Almost every Friday we did Physical Training PT, yes, I had to do it too. By the time I graduated my rank was a Master Sergeant, and I had about 20 ribbons and awards, that I earned over the years.

Also, in school, I took other elective classes like; web design. Web 1; nothing but HTML coding and Web 2; using Adobe Dreamweaver. I don't like HTML coding; it takes a lot of work. With HTML, codes must be exactly precise, one forgotten symbol or mistake in typing can make your site look bad. There have been countless times where I've had to look and relook for 20 minutes at my code to fix one issue.

I enjoy using Adobe Dreamweaver for web design, and I used it again in college. I also took a graphic arts class. I was a member of Future Business Leaders of America (FBLA) and a peer mediator for a short time.

My senior year I was on my yearbook staff. I designed about 6 pages of my senior yearbook. I also went to Homecoming and Prom both my junior and senior year. Also, each year I went to the military ball, JROTC dance.

All the JROTC programs in the county went to the ball. At the ball, guys had to wear class A's, a military dress uniform, I enjoyed dressing up in class A's, and girls wore dresses. I remember one year I had a date to this, but for some reason, she couldn't make it. I was kind of down when my date didn't show.

Four months before I was eighteen this foster mother kicked me out. Because of my behavior and running away. This foster mom didn't treat me like I was seventeen, I believed and still do, some of her rules and comments towards me were uncalled for and hurt me. For example; I had a room to myself and sometimes couldn't have my door closed at night. She made me feel like; pleasing myself, was the worst thing in the damn world.

Also, this crazy woman kept saying that I'm borderline mentally retarded. I don't think she would have said that if she'd seen my web design and graphic arts classwork. Also, I had a bedtime, 9 o'clock, every night, if I had nothing going on. Lastly, she kept pushing the saying that she had a genius IQ, I believe that to be a load of crap.

However, despite our differences, we did bond in one way. That one way was TV, I like reality shows like; Big Brother and Survivor, it all started living with this foster mother, we both watched the two every time they were on. She'd even bend on her dumb bedtime rule for a season finale of a show we were watching. One other show I grew to like and watched a lot was American Idol.

I felt treated like a little kid a lot by this woman, so we argued a lot. At 17 after 5 years in this home she kicked me out and I moved to a therapeutic group home ran in collaboration with PEMHS. They had a point system like the other program, but we had more freedom. I got along well there and hardly ever got in trouble, but one time I got into trouble when I tried to run away. At the time, I was finishing the tenth grade and was able to continue going to my regular school. I stayed in this group home for five months.

After turning eighteen, I still had a caseworker with DCF. I was a part of their transition program. They help and work with young adults that age out of the foster system until they turn twenty-one.

I remember one evening we had a get together I attended, and after the get together I stayed in the office for a few hours. I needed help retrieving my birth certificate from my files, so, my caseworker and I then looked through my files for it.

I had eight very thick files, in one, we came across a birthday card from my grandmother from when I was ten years old. Don't remember how I felt, but I took it with me.

With the program, you have a social worker and receive a monthly allowance if you are active in any educational program. Also because of aging out of foster care, I received a waiver to go to a Florida public college until my bachelor's or my twenty-eighth birthday.

Also, I got set up on the Medicaid waiver program because of my disability, so I have a helper that helps with things I may need, like; grocery shopping, getting to doctors, and other things. I still am on the Medicaid waiver program as I'm writing this book but, my independence has improved, and you will see as you read on.

I moved to an assistive living home when I turned eighteen. Shortly after I moved in, I got a bit of money and was able to get my first cell phone. Back in my foster home, I was not allowed to have a cell phone;

I hated that. I was like the only one out of all my friends in school that didn't have a cell phone. The cell phone was just a basic pre-paid minute phone

Around this same time, I had a guardian ad-Leiden mentor who would hang out with me. We'd meet up a lot, going to; the movies, malls, and Ray's baseball games. He had season tickets to the games, so from 2008 to 2010, I'd go to at least 15 games with him a year. Also, the JROTC teacher would even hang out with me and provide rides for after-school activities. One time he took me to a UCF football game.

I stayed in the assistive living home for about eleven months. I felt so out of touch there.

I was the youngest resident, and my mentality was way higher than anyone else there. I was first in their primary place in Safety Harbor, for about six months, so I had an hour bus ride to school.

During the time I was in this place I was hardly there. I had very little in common with the residents. So, I wanted to be there as little as possible. I went to Countryside mall all the time; I'd go right after I got off the school bus. I'd ride a scooter for hours around the mall and I made some friends there.

After a bit, a lot of people who worked in the mall knew me by name. I went their every day until I moved.

I moved to their Pinellas Park place by my request. But there, little did I know, they required everyone to be out by 7 am on weekdays, most residents went to day programs, I did not.

In the summer of 2007, all I did during the day was ride the buses and go to the malls. Countryside mall was my favorite at the time. One day, I was riding and met these girls, we quickly became friends. So instead of me being by myself or at the assistive living home, I was with them. I stayed the night most times, went pool hopping, and had my first drink.

Towards the end of the summer, I flew up to Georgia to see my brother, and I stayed up there for two weeks. It was great to get to see my brother again, after 4 years.

In August, I started my senior year. And right before I did, I got to move out of the assistive living home, and in with a family. Honestly, the family I moved in with was my guardian ad-Leiden workers family. They were friendly and very welcoming, I had a lot of freedom too, come on I was nineteen. I stayed there for a little while. I went to the movies and the mall a lot, and I had a charge account with a cab company.

I went back up to Georgia for Christmas, and everyone I grew up with was there, I felt like I was back home. That was my first Christmas with them since 2000. I flew back home New Year's Eve. When I came back, I still stayed with the same family I was with before I left. I was getting ready for the last semester of my senior year.

I had some friends in high school, but the only time we'd see each other was at school, I didn't have anyone to chill with when I wasn't at school, why did I call these people friends? Because they were not, they were just people I saw in school. I started going to the local mall, Tyrone mall, a lot because it was just something to do. Soon most of the people who worked in the mall knew me by name. I'd become what you'd call a mall rat. For hours a day, I'd ride around the mall in a scooter. And I most of the time had a soda from

Chick-Fil-A in my hand. On days I had money I had

Sbarro's because pasta is my favorite thing to eat

One day I met a beautiful girl who worked at a

kiosk, and we began talking a lot. After a few weeks we

were best friends, we were always hanging out. At

work, if she had no customers, we just sat there and

chatted. At this time, she was the only friend I had, so I

very much liked spending time with her. I was a senior

in High School but had no one to hang out with. She

was a few years older than me and not in school. She

had a car, so when she worked, she drove me home a

lot when she got off, and on days she wasn't working,

we went to dinner or lunch and the movies. One day she

even let me try to drive her car in a big empty parking

lot, I did ok provided it was a stick.

We got to know each other well. However, she had a boyfriend; and he was always out of town working. One night, we went to dinner and a movie, at this point we were hanging out for like four months, I got caught up in the moment as we were sitting in the theater and asked, "Can I put my arm around you." She said, no.

The next day she said, on a phone call "I don't appreciate you hitting on me. We can't be friends anymore." I was crushed and wasn't trying to hit on her, I thought, so I just lost my best friend, and my only friend. I was very depressed for weeks, and one night, I got home late from a movie and the family got very mad. So at that point, I couldn't take it anymore.

They said in the morning I was to pack up all my stuff because were kicking you out. As they returned to their room, I grabbed all my medication and ate every pill. I nearly succeeded in killing myself. I passed out and remembered seeing that I was in an ambulance, for a second. I was completely out of it. I had to have my stomach pumped and was in and out of sleep for days. After leaving the hospital, I went to another assistive living home for three weeks, then got a place of my own.

I moved in three days before I graduated from Dixie M. Hollins High School on June 3, 2008. It was a 500sq studio in Downtown St. Petersburg. A bit after moving in, I started walking around in downtown St. Petersburg on Friday and Saturday nights.

One night a manager of a lobby bar let me hang out, provided I can only drink soda because I'm under twenty-one, I was nineteen. But I soon became a regular there. For months, my regular Friday routine was to be at Tyrone mall until close, then ride the bus to downtown and go to the lobby.

In August of that same year, I started going to an educational program for people who graduated high school with a special diploma. It was easy, too easy for me. But I didn't quite know what I wanted to do with my life just yet.

One of the teachers knew my situation, I believe I told her. Around Thanksgiving she let me spend it with her and her family. It was nice to have someone do this for me. I went to the mall after she dropped me off. I wanted to see what Black Friday was really like so, I was at Tyrone mall from 9 pm to 8 am, the mall didn't open till 4 am. At 7 am I went back to my apartment to get some rest, but 4 pm I was up and soon back out.

One day when I was roaming the mall, I met a girl who worked there, she invited me out with her after she got off work. We when to a store, back to her place and then, out on the town. She paid for everything, provided at the time I had no money. This night was completely unexpected. I was twenty, but she snuck me in the club with her.

After the club, we took a cab to get some food and then back to her place; I stayed the night there even though I lived in my place blocks away. That night I lost my virginity. After that night, we played house for like a week. I didn't want it to end, but it did. And when it did end, I didn't know why. I was down because I thought she was really into me. After like two weeks of her not responding anymore I let it go.

In the summer of 2009, I heard about a program that I qualified for, and that had my interest, the program was IT summer camp put on through WorkNet Pinellas. We got $250 a week for attending, we had to be there 9 to 4:30 Monday through Thursday, and we were working in-depth with Microsoft Office. We learned all the ins and outs of the office suite.

One day, the staff asked me, "Are you in college?" No, I replied. "Your work is great, you need to go to college, you can do it," they said. Them saying that was possibly the first time in my life someone told I could do something, and it made me think; "Why should I not do something just because someone said I can't." I took it conversation to heart and it possible that this one conversation changed my life.

Hell, the foster mother I was with as a teenager told me repeatedly, "You'll never be able to go to college." Even my high school guidance counselor said college might not be for me. Well, I have a special diploma, I said to the staff. I was told to get my GED so that I could go to college, I did just that. In the summer of 2010, I went to the IT camp again.

For a little, while I attended a church regularly,
it was right across from the mall. The church people
approached me in the mall and asked me to come check
out their church. I liked it and was kind of focused on
what they were preaching. Some stuff made more sense
to me than others, and I can't say that I lived or will live
strictly by the word of God, but I believe in him. I was
blessed with cash in my pocket almost every time I
attended by a couple, but it wasn't why I went.

In August 2009, I entered a GED program. The
learning center was in walking distance of my
apartment, I went 4 to 6 hours at 3 to 4 day a week.
Within nine months I moved up six reading and seven
math grade levels, and after eleven months, I graduated
from the program.

I also started working at a local café part-time, I was a busboy. The restaurant was like 500 feet away from my apartment. I got paid under the table; I worked a few hours a week for like $60 to $120 a week.

I worked for the café for about 8 months and got paid under the table. However, I got fired for mothing off to the owner after doing a few extra hours and not getting more money. So, after being fired started to hustle by selling soda's and cigarettes', I believe one day, within the first week, I made $150 a day. I did this hustle for about a month. Also, a cell phone kiosk gave me accessories to sell at the bus stop at the mall, I did that for like a month. I also made friends that worked at an AT&T kiosk and hung out with them a couple of times.

I turned twenty-one and was excited, and being that I lived downtown, I started going out a lot to bars and clubs on Friday and Saturday nights. After a few weeks of going out every weekend, one night I met a girl, and we became friends. At first, I liked her as more than a friend, but she saw me as a younger brother. Within two weeks we were hanging out daily, and I was staying over most nights.

I quickly became friends with one of her best friends and her boyfriend, and her. This friendship lasted for about sixteen months We had a huge party on New Year's Eve, but I took my limit too far and ended up in the ER. They were still my friends after that but wanted me to go easier on my drinking. Our friendship did go a year later; we just lost contact.

After being on my own for a year and a half and having cable subscriptions and a cell phone in my name, I became obsessed with; Cable TV, Internet, and Cell Phone services, and I started to compare them all. I got fliers from every provider to compare them. I had had the big two cable providers in my area and at this point been with three different cell phone providers. I started collecting all the information I could on all providers. '

I took the gathered information plus my personal experience and made a website; The Service Finder. At first, it only compared TV, Internet, and Home Phone services in the Tampa Bay region, plus the major cell phone providers. I dreamed that my web site would be big, but it wasn't.

Then I branched it out to about ten major areas in the U.S. The site was active for about five years, and I did frequent updates. For marketing, I had business cards and flyers made, sometimes, I'd ride the busses all day over town with them. I also had a Facebook page for it and shared it through my personal Facebook. However, with all my efforts I failed to get a lot of hits on my web site. It was costing me time and a bit of money, but I was getting nothing out of it.

Chapter Three:

Marriage

I hated being single, so, I put an ad on Craigslist looking for a girlfriend. Within a few weeks of my posting, I got what I was looking for. However, it wasn't her that found my ad. Her sister was on the site looking for a boat and just took a quick look at the personals section. The sister then convinced her, my ex, to reach out to me.

We sent a few emails back and forth over a few days, then started talking on the phone. She lived 45 minutes from me in Brandon. Our first meet was at a mall in Tampa, we met and liked each other.

We then talked more and more, less than a month later we started dating. Most of the time I went there, to Brandon, I stayed at her mom's house with her. She stayed with her mom being that she has some challenges. Also, one of her close friends let us stay at her place some weekends.

Her friend soon got jealous that my girlfriend was giving me more attention than her. So, she started calling my phone private acting like I was messing around with another girl, as an attempt to break us up. I got a new apartment in St. Petersburg two weeks before we met.

My new apartment was bigger and nicer than my old one, however, not in downtown. By the time I got this apartment I had a TV and could afford cable. My new apartment was a one-bedroom and bath, and I had my living room and bedroom fully furnished.

We saw each other almost every week Friday to Sunday. I was going to school at the GED program or St. Petersburg College (SPC), Monday to Thursday. We didn't have sex until after our engagement, which was after seven months of dating, but she was ok

with laying naked together after dating for about a

month. So, we were able to touch and see each other.

In the eleven months that I was in St. Petersburg, as

we were dating, she came over to my place like twice,

the first time we had sex was at my home. However,

her parents were furious when it did happen, and we

went a week without seeing each other, which we both

hated. We started seeing each other every week after

that and had sex every chance we got.

In the summer of 2010, I graduated from the GED,

and I started at SPC that fall. Two weeks later, on my

twenty-second birthday, my girlfriend and

I got engaged. As it got closer to my move, I started transferring all my schooling stuff from SPC to Hillsborough Community College (HCC). It took weeks and a lot of time. Six times in a few months I rode the bus 7 hours from my place in St. Petersburg to HCC.

On New Year's Day, I moved to Riverview. We got a 2 bed 2 bath apartment, in which I'm living currently in by myself. Two weeks later I started HCC and three weeks later, on February 4th, 2011, I got married. I invited my brother, along with his parents, to come down from Georgia to my wedding. They came down, and my brother was a part of my wedding as my best man.

For our honeymoon, we went to Disney for four days. My wife's sister and boyfriend went with us to help take us around and assist with other things.

My marriage was good for like the first year, maybe a year and a half, but then we just argued too much, plus her family got overly involved, and she got too lazy. Now my wife is intelligent and was a University of South Florida (USF) student, but there were some life choices she wasn't smart on making.

When we had first got together, she had a helper that got her to the point to where she was more independent than she has ever been before. I saw her improvement, but, the second she lost that worker, her independence went too. I then began starting to help with just about everything; from taking care of her to household chores. I didn't like doing everything, but I did it because I truly loved her.

When she first began her master's degree online, I was also required to help with that. Knowing how we argued and all the things I had to do, she wanted to add a baby too. The only three things I did wrong, to some, not to others, was watching porn, drinking beer, and sometimes breaking my shit out of anger. Even when I was married, I still liked to go out to bars and the mall.

At times, my wife and I went two to three weeks

without having sex. I was just worn out at times; I did most of the work when we made love. However, I did love her and liked her pussy. We did it as much as I could, sometimes she wanted it more than me.

There was a bar within walking distance of our apartment. I was a regular there and went at least once a week. The one night I wanted to go was Tuesday, because they had karaoke there, I loved doing karaoke. I went to that bar week after week for years. One night the floor was wet, I slipped and fell. I was cut off but didn't agree with the reasoning.

I proceeded to get beer from others and was disrespectful to the bartender.

I then got banned for life from that bar, still, as I'm writing this, seven years later, they won't let me in.

I always asked my wife if she wanted to join me because I like going out a lot, she just chose not to go. Her family began to always put doubts in her head about me, like, I was not faithful to her. She sometimes believed it. She didn't stand up to them about me and what she truly felt.

My wife was a big sports fan, she liked and watched every sport except NASCAR, golf, and basketball. I took her to every sporting event in the area, as much as we could afford. The reason why is because I knew she liked it, so I wanted to make my wife happy.

My wife and I were both going to school and getting money from it, but besides rent and electric, I had to use mine for all the bills. However, she used hers for whatever she wanted. If I wanted to get something, I wanted I had to ask, she didn't. The cable we both used, but she didn't even put in $20 a month, but she wanted to have a cable package that had her shows, but however, I did at times charge up to $50 for adult programming on the bill but paid it. When we both agreed on getting a brand new $1200-bedroom set, the cost was all on me.

The arguing between us was getting old and got worse and worse, and it hurt. When we let other members of her family stay with us, a few times, nothing was kept just between my wife and me.

Witch, in turn, demolished our marriage. I got a job in May 2012 at a Casino in Tampa, as an Employee Dining Room Attendant. Me having this job began to piss my wife off. She wanted to work but had trouble finding a job.

She was also upset that I had the job while I was still in school and she just got her degree, but nobody had hired her yet. About eight months after having this job I found out that a bunch of people from work hung out together after work.

On Sunday's after work a lot of them went out to the same bar; I started going out too. I made a lot of friends at this time, some my age and some older.

These friends are still here for me as I'm writing this, five years later. One has become like an older brother to me. My wife was always invited to join me. The casino had yearly talent shows, on a local and state level. State show was healed at the casino in Hollywood, FL. My wife always accompanied me to both shows. So yes, my co-workers saw her and knew I was married.

On our third wedding anniversary, she said: "I've been jealous of your job, I keep thinking you're going to find someone better at work and leave me." I was upset, "why would I do that?" I asked her. I do not look for other people while I'm with someone. That got me really upset and I had a lot of anger building up over the following days. With all my anger built up I broke a new TV I'd just got like three weeks before.

We got separated a day later, on February 6th, 2014, I was hurt, but at the same time tired of it all. I felt like I couldn't do anything right no matter what. I also felt very underappreciated by her. I even took my wedding ring off and chucked it at the wall. I had a mixture of sadness and angry feelings. I did want us to work out and I really believe I tried, but I couldn't anymore.

Every time we got into a big argument, she left, and I was alone at home for a few days. Before we separated, I agreed to go to six marriage counseling sessions. I tried to listen to the counselor's advice, but, the second I saw she wasn't, I didn't. An example was for me to cut back on drinking while she cuts back on family involvement, her family saw still overly involved so I did what I wanted.

The separation happened a few weeks after the start

of my last semester before graduating from HCC. After

this, I just worked a lot and went out all the time. I fell

two weeks behind in school, but my teachers

understood and were ok with me turning in late work.

They even referred me to the school counseling center.

I went there weekly. After a month, my wife came

back just for a place to stay for two months. It was

awkward. I stayed home as little as possible.

One night right after my separation I worked till

late, a coworker drove me home, she's not into guys,

but she put on porno and jacked me off, two weeks later

we had intercourse, we are still friends today and at

times have hooked up.

On May 5TH, 2014, I graduated from HCC with an A.S. Degree in Web Design. To complete my degree, I had to find a client to build a website for. My client was 0a DJ I knew from a local bar. It was nice having a degree, and I was very proud of myself. I was alone outside of work all summer, so I began hanging out with people in my neighborhood, wasn't the best crowd, but I was lonely.

On July 13th I got divorced, my wife didn't even show up to court. I took it hard and the rest of the year was rough and lonely. For years after our marriage, we occasionally hooked up. Four months after the divorce she reached out to me for a booty call, asking me to be friends with benefits, we hooked up within months after our divorce. We also hooked over the years following our divorce. The most recent time was years later, January 2018, right after I went through my last break-up, which you will read about later.

My ex-wife was my first girlfriend and my first real love. I'm always going to remember her and all my exes you will read about and have some level of love for them. However, out of all my exes, my ex-wife hurt me the least.

Chapter Four:

After Marriage

I applied for USF that summer but got denied
because of a math grade. I was eligible to graduate
HCC with one D because I was in an applied science
degree. However, this rule has changed since then. My
one D was in college algebra, however, to admit into

USF, I needed one college-level math with a C or

better. So, the fall of 2014 I went back to HCC for one

semester.

Math was the most challenging subject,

especially Algebra. It was like learning a second

language to me. It was just hard for me to understand.

In every semester at HCC, I was in a math class. I took

Beginning Algebra twice, and Intermediate Algebra

three times, I was in each one for a full eighteen-week

semester.

In the fall of 2014, my semester at school was

hard, because I let this dumb ass roommate move in.

Now I wanted a few house parties, but the roommate

took it out of control. I had parties at my house almost every night; I'd sometimes get home and see random people in my apartment unexpectedly. All the parting started to bother me a lot, and I tried to tone it down. However, my roommate didn't care and always ignored my wishes. It's like they just took over my own house like it was their own, and never helped me out with a single bill. He thought just because he bought me beers that was good enough.

I had trouble studying and doing homework for school. I cut my arm one night because I was so mad, I had a failed marriage, a roommate who was disrespectful, and I couldn't do well in most classes. My roommate, however, didn't change to make life easier for me.

But I got through it, got the B in math, in January got the roommate out and started USF.

I started using dating sites, apps and Craigslist. I use Craigslist to give me a hookup, believe it or not easily, I had about six different women in two years hook up with me, and I didn't even pay a dime. So I had a pretty good thing going, I was single and still getting some action here and there.

One time a hook up happened between classes, I had a 3-hour break, and she picked me up from school. I'm still on the dating sites and apps as I'm writing this. I've been on them for the past four and a half years on and off.

When I'm in a relationship, I'm off them. One year I was lucky and got with six different women.

In March 2015, I met a new girl online and started dating. We dated for about six weeks, and I went to see her in Zephyrhills every chance I got. She and I did do "it" on the first night and we really thought we were going to be together for a long time.

I was working for three days and in school for two. I paid my best friend from work $20 to take me to her every other week right after my last class got out, stay the night, and the next day, I took 4 or more busses 9 hours home through 3 counties.

There was one time I stayed for two days. She and I spent a day with my friends from work going to Adventure Island and a local bar. That was fun. And we did a lot. About two days later, on her bus back home broke up with me for no reason, she wasn't thinking and regretted it for years. We even hooked up at times after we weren't together.

In the summer, I move one of my old roommates' back in, I wanted the company, and he was like a brother to me, so I thought. I also had my first ever vacation scheduled off work. Originally it was for June, but because work needed me to stay, so it was postponed for July.

I went for seven days to South Beach, Miami. I left on a Tuesday taking the mega bus. It was $1 each way, but I paid $29 because I missed my scheduled departure, which was in the morning. The bus ride was 5 and a half hours and took me from Downtown Tampa to Miami Airport. From the airport, I took bus 150 the Miami Beach flyer. I had trouble finding my hostel and got lost; a nice man helped me by walking around with me to find my hostel. I stayed at Bikini Hostel on West Avenue and 13 Street. The Hostel was $15 per night and had a full café & bar.

The first night I wanted to go out for a drink, I found one of the cheapest coolest bars in South Beach, Lost Weekend. They have pictures of beer for $14; most bars charge $7 for one beer.

The next day I went to a beach, now I consider myself a nudist at heart, so after searching the internet with my phone, I was happy I found an optional clothing beach, just north of Bel Harbor.

Haulover Beach is a part of Miami and has a half-mile nude section. I was there for 5 hours, on Wednesday. You think being naked on a beach with others would feel weird, am I right? Well, to me not really. The complete opposite, very freeing and relaxing. When I found a spot, I right away took off all my clothes.

Thursday, I stayed at the Hard Rock Hotel & Casino in Hollywood, FL. The room was very nice with a great view. I got a discounted rate because I work for the company. I drank a lot through the night; I also met up with a friend from back home that I hadn't seen in years. I gambled a bit and finally went into my room around 4 am.

I checked back into Bikini Hostel on Friday, after spending 5 hours at Haulover Beach. That night I went to a club called Mansion. The club promoter that visits the hostels gave me free admission. We road in a limo from the Hostel to the club but had to find our way back. The club was huge and something I've never seen, beer was $13, so I only had 2 and left after just an hour and a half in the club.

I went back to Haulover Beach that Saturday and spent the entire day, I met some people on this day and spent a while talking with them. They even offered me a ride to my Hostel. That night I met a group of people at the hostel. After like an hour of hanging out, they said, "We are going out," they ask me to go with them. I said, "I couldn't spend any more money," they said, "We got you covered." I went.

We walked 45 minutes from one side of South Beach to th1e other. We went to one club for 2 hours and had a VIP table. Then we all followed one guy who wanted to go to a gay bar; we were there until 4:45 in the morning, a few people and myself were exhausted, we ubered back to the hostel while some people walked back and stayed for the last 15 minutes. Sunday, I went to Haulover Beach again and Monday I took the bus back to Tampa.

After traveling this first time, I had an eye-opening experience. I was nervous at first, but that went away in a few days. This trip opened me up and made me want to travel more.

Who knew? Someone with my disability could travel completely alone, more than 200 miles away from their home. Being in a hostel for the first time was scary at first, but I got to meet people and interact with people.

I then knew that if I'd travel again, I'd choose to stay at a hostel.

In November, I started chatting with a girl online, we exchanged numbers quickly, and we talked on and off for months, in the meantime, with her ok, I continued my travels.

Towards the end of December of 2015, I went to New York City for New Year's Eve. I flew there; the first night, I had a big problem finding the hostel, but it wasn't a hostel anyway; it was just a guy renting out a room in his apartment.

I contacted the travel provider that I used for my booking, and they gave me some credits, so my first night in NYC some girl let me crash, in her spare room, so I wasn't on the street.

I was able to find hostels for the remainder of my trip. One hostel I had my room behind a locked door, but the room was no more than twenty square feet. I was only in NYC for five days.

I spent a lot of time in Time Square, where I went to Dave N' Busters quite a bit. The Dave N Busters in New York City was the first location I've visited.

I took the bus system only a couple of times because I mostly used the subway to get around. I visited Central Park and Washington Square Park. I also went on a tour bus and went to see a movie.

I was in a club in the middle of the city on New Year's Eve. At the club, we got a few free drinks and an hour of food with admission. My time in NYC was an excellent experience, except for the first night.

My last night, I lost my ID, so, I had to go through a lot of paperwork and a bit more security measures to get my plane back home. I got back home and went on with my life, with school, work, etc.

I made a big mistake by signing up for seven classes and soon regretted it. One of my classes was sign language, I took it for about 3 weeks, but it was extremely difficult so. I dropped it, I did then a petition to wave my foreign language requirement, and won, so other classes substituted that requirement. I also got wrapped up in the girl 1 was talking to before I left. Between January and March, we talked on and off, because of her crazy self.

One week after she had me already hooked, she said, "Let's stop talking, I have cancer, I can't get serious." So, I honored what she said; we had no communication for two weeks.

Then she starts messaging me again. She wants me and doesn't have cancer. For my next trip, I wanted to do it for spring break, so I did.

My spring break was eleven days or so after my best friend's / roommate's birthday, so I paid for him to go with me. We went down to Miami from Tampa for a week; it started well for both of us at first. However, he spent a little too much money within the first two days.

On our second or third day there we went to the Hollywood hard rock casino and Hooters, we spent more. By the fourth day, we were just about broke. I spent every free minute talking to the girl for hours on end.

For example, I'd be walking on the beach with the phone on my ear. For hours every day, we talked. We both were into each other and couldn't wait to meet.

I had $80 and 2 more days in Miami, but I sent her $20 so she and her daughter could eat. We were going to be together, and I bought her a bus ride to Tampa, she'd arrive two days after I returned from my vacation in Miami.

When she arrived, I had my best friend from work take me to go pick her up at a bus station in downtown Tampa, seeing her for the first time was amazing. As we rode in the car to my apartment, we held hands and smiled at one another. We were very much infatuated with one another.

Meanwhile, in Miami, my friend lost control and got himself kicked out of the hostel we were staying in, so my money for his bed went down the drain. He had no room for the rest of the trip; we had like four more days. I was a bit upset that he could not control himself, but however, he got bad news from family back home. At the time of his outburst, I was not there, I was miles up the road at my favorite beach. My friend and I would hang out at night, outside of the hostel and during the day I'd be up to the road at the nude beach. When we returned home, my friend moved out. He wasn't on the lease, so I was told by my landlord to put him out. I had a problem with moving people in who were on my lease, after my marriage I was the only person on the lease in this apartment. It was a 2 bed 2 bath and I could afford it on my own, but I liked the idea of trying to make extra money and having company. Most times this old best-friend did pay me $165-$225 every 2 weeks for the room, and he was the only person that gave me cash regularly for his room.

My girl came two days later. And I'd start a six month on/off relationship that I'd regret. At first, I'm feeling great, the school's going well, work is too, and I got my girl and her daughter at home. My girlfriend knew I liked to be naked and it didn't bother her. She was even topless or fully nude for hours on end, sometimes a full day.

The plan was for her to come visit me for one week; she had an apartment 2 hours away, but after the first few days she decided to stay permanently. We were pleased to be together and had sex every day; I never wanted it to end; the first two weeks were great between her and me, and we loved every minute of each other's company. After two weeks of it just being her and I, my friend would start coming back to the house to chill, even if I wasn't there, he'd hang out in my place with my girl.

The arguments soon started between my girlfriend and me, and most of the time they were over nothing. Within a few weeks, my girl said she needed to rethink things. I was never under the impression that we were broke up and it was never explicitly stated.

A day or two later, on Mother's Day, she left. I bought her a $90 worth of flowers from pro-flowers, I went to work, expected her to be there, but when I returned home from work, she wasn't. I also found a love note on my bed ¬from her to my friend. The person whom I considered to be like a brother, was now with my girl. I called someone; we went to the bar for a few hours, then I returned home.

Then she came back to pretend to check up on me as if she gave a damn and quickly ran back out, I tried to follow her but couldn't keep up. Then I cut myself to try and slit my wrists; I called the police myself to say that I was killing myself. The cut on my wrist was deep enough to leave a scar which is still there today.

A month later my friend messed up with her, she claims she was raped by a friend of him, and she came to ask me to take her back, I didn't want to, but I did. I was crying due to how she hurt me before, and she was pleading for another chance. She said that I was a great guy and she'd never leave me again. She even swears that on her daughter. It started great, almost better than the first time we were together. We went out a lot.

A month later we have one big argument, and most likely it over nothing, she sleeps on the couch at times she deliberately says things to taunt me, and asks, "You mad yet?' After that night, the next day she says; "I'm going for a walk, I promise I'll be back," two days go by no sign of her, her grandmother even calls me to ask where is. The third day I see her with my best friend, she left me again for him.

She came back a month later when I was stuck on bed rest. I burned myself at work, got a second degree burn on my right leg. The burn happened as I was flushing a coffee machine. When my girlfriend came back, Again. It started great for two weeks, like before, but then she started talking to another guy. She did not care how it hurt me she did it anyway. At 2, 3, and 4 in the morning, she was on her phone with this other guy, for an hour or longer. She said, "He's just a friend." But she's talking sexually to him, saying baby, I love you, etc.

Her behavior got worse and she was always thinking a was mad or trying to start a fight. At times when she got mad, she when to the fridge and dumped out all my beer and any food I recently had bought. When she did that I got mad because it was wasting my money, something she didn't think or care about.

One time I grabbed her arm to try and stop her because I got tired of it being a waste of my money and she pushed me hard. When I was on my phone to talk to friends or my social worker about problems, she'd reach to try to take my phone away, one time I tried to do the same to her and she kicked me. She wanted all her people to know about me, but none of my people to know about her.

When I ordered something like pizza for us, she wanted me to order at least $45 worth. We could have ordered $25 worth, but she always wanted extra. We were ordering delivery every week or so. But when she got mad most of the order went into the trash.

She tried to accuse me of abuse and even called the police on me. The last time she called they made her leave, and that was the end of our relationship, she was still mean to me on the phone and Facebook. She tried to say I was stocking her, but It was the other way around.

She went through one of my coworkers and used her sister's Facebook to send me messages because

I blocked her on Facebook and changed my phone

number. Since more lies had spread, like me messaging

everyone in her family about her, I stopped using

Facebook altogether for three months.

Also, around this time, I started hanging out

with people in my apartment complex. It was nice, and,

in the beginning, they made me feel like they were real

friends. The friendship lasted a good while, but then

true colors started to show. When it did, I began to hang

out a lot less. I still as I'm writing this, say hi,

occasionally, but I don't hang out as I did before.

I started talking to someone else a week after

my girl, and I split; she was homeless living in her

friend's van. Her friend was some old guy, and she swears he was only her friend. Within the first six weeks I told her everything, she seemed very friendly, supportive and understanding, but soon, that would change.

We got together six weeks later, and I moved her in. We stayed together for three months. The entire time I came second to her best friend all because she wanted to keep hold of the van. I never got to meet this friend of hers.

Meanwhile, she made me move a couple into my place, which was the biggest mistake ever. Most of the time they didn't clean up after themselves, and they thought they could talk to me any way they wanted. My girlfriend didn't even stick up for me. Every Saturday she was out with her best friend while I was alone, she also stayed in motels with him twice. But she couldn't share a room with me, her boyfriend. She was very controlling with me.

At times my girlfriend got right up in my face and yelled at me, sometimes to the point to where I thought she was going to hit me. One day I said something like; "You're using me," I said that as I was standing on the opposite side of the living room. she then charged at me, I ran into my room and she followed. She cornered me in my own closet and started hitting me. I repeatedly said stop, she didn't, so I bit her in defense.

I spent about $6,000 in the three months on her and house improvements for her, most of it was student loans form my school. In December, she went to see her brother in California; I paid for her to go because I wanted her to have a chance to see him. I know how it feels to go without seeing siblings for a while, so that's why I offered. We argued over text message, and she never came back.

The argument started because my landlord came over and said the couple living in my house was not on my lease, therefore they had to go. My ex-had their side, not mine and could care less if I lost my place. My ex-strong armed me to move these people in knowing it wasn't legally allowed and could wind up getting me evicted. She said she loved me and wanted to be with me, but in our relationship, her actions did not back up what she was telling me. So, I once again was single.

In January 2017, I started my last semester at USF. I had only three online classes. I found one of them to be harder than expected and another to be just frustrating. The course that was hard didn't measure up to my ideal. And no matter how well I thought I did, I didn't get above a C on a single assignment. In the other class, we were in a group the entire time. My group had communication issues.

For my last spring break, I went down to Miami; I flew down right after work. This time I did not go to

Hollywood Hard Rock, instead, I just stayed on the beach. I hung out on South Beach and the nudist beach a lot during the day. At night I was at either a bar or club.

One afternoon I went on a party boat, where we were taken to a private island and had a cookout with soda, beer, and wine. It was so much fun, and well worth $65.00. I made some friends and had a lot of fun. We played a game of flip cup on the island; there was about 16 of us in the game. I went to the nudist beach a few times.

I went to hang out on South Beach a few times, and it was lively. All the college students packed one small section of the beach. The beach stretches for a few miles, but only like a block was packed, the same area, every day. After spring break, I just had five weeks of school left, and five weeks until graduation.

On the 6th of May, I walked in the graduation ceremony graduating with my bachelor's degree in Information Technology. I had a big party at a bar the next evening, about 50 people from work showed up, I thanked them all and had a lot of fun.

I've always wanted to go to Los Angela's, CA. and right after graduation I did. It was my gift to myself for getting my bachelor's degree. I left Orlando airport at about 3:30 P.M. on Thursday, May 11th, one of my

supervisors gave me a ride. I went for a week and a

half, with three days spent in San Diego.

My first full day I toured the Dolby Theater,

where the Oscars are held and took a trolley tour around

Hollywood. With the next two days being the weekend,

I just explored.

On Saturday, I walked around a mall for a few

hours and then went to Venice Beach. And Sunday I

didn't do much besides grocery shopping, staff from

my hostel was kind enough to give me a ride to and

from a grocery store.

The Hostel I stayed at was very nice, unlike a Hostel I've been at before. It was a mansion with a guest house. The staff there was friendly and excellent, so was the owner, whom I met. I also made some friends almost instantly.

I toured two studios while I was in LA.; Sony Pictures on Monday, May 15th, and Warner Bros. on Tuesday, May 16th. I visited Santa Monica after the tour on Monday but didn't stay their long. And Tuesday I went to Hollywood after my tour. The tours were excellent; I have mad respect for all who create movies and TV. It takes a lot of hard work, long hours, and creativity to make a TV show and movie.

To save money I didn't do much on Wednesday, I just stayed at the hostel, also on that day I announced on Facebook that I was writing a book. I started writing my first book; Life is One Steep Cliff. I spent hours on a computer in the Hostels office, just writing away. In that one day, I'd written a few pages.

Thursday, I checked out Long Beach but was only there for a very short time. I went to San Diego that Friday. I stayed in a nice hostel and made a friend right away. The hostel was nice and at a great spot in downtown San Diego.

That night I went out to a prime location downtown. On Saturday, I went to check out a nudist beach, that someone at a nudist beach in Miami mentioned. It was tough to get to; I was warned to access this beach, I had to walk down a 300-foot cliff. I stayed at the beach for a few hours. Then that night I went out again. I did nothing on Sunday.

My flight back home was Monday night. About 1:30 pm, I returned to LA from San Diego. I stayed in the Hollywood area for about 6 hours. Hanging out at Hard Rock Cafe, Hooters, and Dave N' Busters. I spent about $40 in all three places total in food and drinks. I met some people at the bar at Dave N' Busters, one of them took a picture with me and offered to pay for some of my drinks. For my first time in LA, I liked it and I had a plan to move to LA within the next 2 years, I even told people I meet in the hostel my plan to move.

At about 7:45 I got the Metro Rail and headed to the airport. I got to LAX at about 9:15 pm. On my way to the airport I deliberately took my time, I wanted to miss my flight, and hated the thought of going back home. However, I made my flight that was due to leave at 10:10, was delayed and left at 10:45. Not too long after take-off, I was crying, what can I say, I hated Tampa, FL. I got back to Orlando airport at 6:45 the following morning. A friend of mine came to give me a ride back home from Orlando but didn't get there until like 10 am.

In August I met a girl, she seemed very nice, we talked and met once within the first six weeks of getting to know, because I was in the middle of planning a

Vegas trip for my birthday. I took my best friend with me on my Vegas trip because I knew she needed a break from stuff at home.

We were in Vegas for four days. I spent about $1100 on; playing, food, drinking, shows, and transportation. The show I went to showed a lot of boobs. After Vegas, I was planned to go to Miami Beach, but it changed due to a Hurricane. In October I started my master's degree online at the University of Phoenix.

Chapter Five:

The One-Person Relationship

August 18TH, 2017. I'm online looking at dating options, and I'm using a handful of dating sites and apps. As I'm browsing, I go on my E-Harmony account. I received a wink back from someone who caught my eye a day or two ago. We then exchange a handful of messages, as we were, I was also on my way to a meetup event through Match.

As the day progresses so does the conversation on E Harmony. I go to the Match event that evening and focus on both, the event and online. However, I found myself focused more on the online conversation I was having.

As days pass, we on E Harmony talk more and more, and it was great how much we had in common. We soon exchange numbers and get off the line. As we keep talking, I ask her to read a book, Life Is One Steep Cliff, which is 55% of what you have read up until now, that I had recently finished.

She was really into me after reading it. As we talk more, I was very upfront with her about my habits and how I think after a few months sex should be a part of a growing relationship.

Three months sounded reasonable to both of us. She said, "Any more than three months is expecting too much."--Note I quoted that. Did I want it to happen in less than six weeks? Yes, but I had strong feelings for her and decided to bend on that. However, I was four months without sex and under sexual frustration. And my last relationship, that lasted three months had no sex.

My thought before getting with her was not to wait. Because, I give a lot in a relationship and should get my needs met, when I give but get nothing, but dumped, that makes me very angry. However, a relationship is way more than sex, and honestly, physical attraction wasn't there for me, but most of the time it doesn't matter.

The emotional attraction was, and that is what matters the most to me. We then arrange a meet at a local mall. We walked through the mall and talked. One conversation was about how job hunting was frustrating. "Don't you hate how these employers make you wait and not be upfront with you?" she said, yes, I said.

That conversation leads to others and from then we wanted to see one another again. The next time we met was three weeks after that because I went to Las Vegas for my birthday.

We had breakfast at a diner, Wolfs Den, near her home. I had just got off working all night. But work needed me for a double shift, so I had 7 am to 9:30 am to go to breakfast, and I did. We saw we had more in common, as we went for a short walk into Sam's Club, she started to hold my hand.

I went back to work and stayed till 2 pm, at 11 pm I was due back for another overnight shift. We talked more and more; we found we had more in common, and we went out again about a week or two later. My girlfriend and I see a movie for a mid-day date. This date was one she chose to keep secret from her mom. We saw flatliners. The film was scarier than it seemed. But we stayed till it was over, even though we debated leaving in the middle.

We exit and wait for our Uber to arrive. "I wish we could have sex, but I might be starting a job soon and very fertile," said my girlfriend. However, it was only our third date, but she had already brought up sex. We take an uber to my home because I want to show her my house.

We get there and start watching TV and chatting a bit. I find out how insecure she is about herself and say; "Your beautiful and perfect the way you are, be you and don't change for nobody." We continue talking, and I share a very dark secret to her.

After 15 minutes, "I've seen your chest, it's only fair if you see mine," she said. Ok now I am shocked, wasn't expecting this. She loses her shirt and pulls her bra down for a few seconds. 5 minutes later, she grabs me and starts kissing me. She instantly felt sparks, she said. We make out, she again exposes her breasts and physically moves my hand to her boob to tell me touching is ok. She leaves soon after to go back home by a specific time, a friend/uber driver was her ride home.

Later that night my friend and I were at a bar. I started crying, everything in my life was going well, I was scared it would be accidentally messed up. I felt like I was the luckiest man alive to have her, messing up was something I never wanted to do. My life has been in and out of hell, and I wasn't used to everything all at once going right, but it was. At this moment I

feel on top of the world, I finally got the girl that was

for me, or so I was tricked into believing.

A few days later, my girlfriend and I are talking;

we start discussing a double date whit a friend of hers

and other topics. She asks me what my turn on was and

then told me hers, being tied up and tickled. She also

expressed that she wanted to make feet tickle videos

and post them on YouTube. We go to lunch that Friday

at Olive Garden, things are still going very well for us.

That following Monday she comes over to try

out the feet tickle. A friend from work and I go pick her

up. We make our first YouTube video and then hang

out. She knows I like to hang out naked and lets me;

she hangs out topless for a bit. She then goes home like an hour later, by an uber, I got for her.

That Friday she comes back over, I send uber to get her. Now I have restraints and feathers that I ordered for her. This time there is no production of a video, I'm naked more, and she's topless more. By her request, I tie her down on my bed. I tickle her for a bit, and then we sit around and look at things on the computer, this is also the day I say, I love you. I couldn't fight it anymore; I did love her very much; I don't think I felt so much in love with anyone before her. That evening we go to Dave N' Busters, we had a great time. And then I get her an uber home. The next day we have a conversation, she wants to push back having sex because she is starting a job. So, after six weeks in this relationship, and making me feel like everything was soon going to happen she wanted to wait. She then proceeds to tell me "It's only about the job, I'm ready but don't want to risk getting pregnant soon after I just start my job." She said ninety days of employment, I asked can we compromise at sixty-five days, she said no.

As days go on, we still talk, but I'm feeling like why it must be all her way like there's no meeting in the middle, I told her my feelings and she said; "Just have sex with someone else, just once, it's ok." I never thought a girlfriend would say that, but, Instantly, I say, no, I'm not cheating on you, and I want to do it with someone I love, you. So, I dropped talking about it for a while.

About a week later she comes over after work; I have an uber pick her up, then we do pizza and Netflix at my place. A few hours later, I get an uber for her to go back home.

A week later we scheduled to have lunch on he lunch break around 12:30. But I'd accidentally oversleep. Being that, I'd just went home from work at about 4 am; I feel so terrible. She is distraught that I stood her up at first, but she then calms down hours later, as she releases that it was a mistake, I do work overnight and need my sleep. I apologized over and over, but she says that it's ok and she understood. By 5 o'clock I take an uber up to wiregrass, which is 30 minutes from my apartment and later that evening, we briefly meet, and that's it.

Throughout the next week, we talk, and I still see if we can continue to progress the physical part in a little less than ninety days, here we are, we've been talking for three months and been together for two. We almost break up because of feeling pressured. Then a day is spent rethinking as she is rethinking the relationship, I think the worst, I do ask my friend who's done it with me before, and who are living with me with her daughters for free if we could have sex. She says no, and nothing happens.

The next day my girlfriend and I don't break up, and it works out. She then tells me "I'm just not ready, I used work because the excuse sounded good, I'm sure by valentine's day I'll be ready for that step," she said, ok, I'll wait I said.

137

We go bowling a week later. At the bowling alley, my girlfriend says, "I'm sorry, after talking with my mom I was in the wrong, I was doing the same as I did in past relationships, I hurt you." We then bowl two games, and after we went to a mall to hang out together a bit more, right now thing seems to be very good between us, I take her home in an uber then I go home.

Around this time, I ask her to consider inviting me for Christmas, I've spent a lot of them alone, and it meant a lot to spend it with her. I cared for her and loved her. She said no, another sign of her not considering me or my feelings at all. I'm thinking if you are with someone that you know has nobody to spend Christmas with, why would you not want to invite them?

The holiday season is rough on me, so, during this time I was in a depressed stage. I have a brother that I haven't seen for close to seven years. For the past three years, I have been alone during the holidays. Being alone during this time always gets me depressed plus I was depressed about the fact that I have a degree, but nobody will give me a chance to work in my field, and, my girlfriend is only thinking about her feelings most of the time.

It began to hurt, and I told her that I felt as if my feelings did not matter to her, I even said in a text, "This is not an equal relationship." A day later, "Ok I'll try to be more understanding" she said. Well, she didn't try being more understanding, as you will see when you read on.

We see each other for dinner two weeks later at Wiregrass. We ate at Moe's, and she paid for our meals, she wanted to, so I let her. We're having conversations about our days were and whatnot. Are you happy? Will we last? I ask. "Don't question it, yes, we're fine. My ex kept questioning the relationship; please don't," she said.

After dinner, we spend about an hour walking around and strolled into a bookstore, where we spent another hour or so. As she's looking at books, I'm right there with her. After a short time, she starts looking at kids books, and says "I have something to tell you." "Tell me," I reply, "I know this might be too soon, but I want to start trying for kids with you soon," she says. I'm now confused, why would she say this, to me?

When she recently told me, she wasn't ready for the physical part of a relationship. Needless to say, when she said that. I knew, without a doubt, this relationship was real. Or so I thought

I get her some books that she is interested in, a couple of them were for her, and a few were for her work. She goes home in an Uber, and I do later, after hanging out at Brass Tap for a few beers.

A week later, Uber picks her up and then me at my job. We go to the mall, and I get a pedicure for her, she said I didn't have to, but I knew she'd like it, so I did. We chill for a few and talk about our future. Do you still think you'll be ready by valentine's day?

I ask, "Actually I'm ready now and I would if I was on birth control or got the pill," she said. I then offer to give her the money for the pill, but she declines.

She gets topless, and we make a topless tickle video for my viewing only. Yes, I did watch it when I was alone and a few times after she dumped me. The video was 15 minutes and we were at my house for like an hour or two. We then left my house and went to Dave N' Busters for the remainder of our time together. She stayed for about an hour before I get her an uber home, and after she's dropped off, I go home myself.

The next Friday we go to Bush Gardens Christmas Town, her mom gave her a ride, this was only the 4th time of about 11 dates she'd have her transportation, one way. We walk through the park, ride the train, and take a few pictures. Everything was great between us, or so I was led to believe.

A friend picks us up about 8 o'clock, and we go hang out at my place. We hung out for an hour or so; I told her I got the pill, the morning-after pill, "Well it's something else, and I don't want to hurt your feelings." She said, tell me. I said I'd rather know. "Ok, the bug problem weirds me out, and that's why I've been pushing sex and staying over."

I have a pest issue no matter how clean I keep the place, as she's watching a movie, I start trying to get my place cleaner. I' m also upset, no matter what and how hard I try, I'm rejected and given excuses constantly on the physical level here.

She keeps coming up with excuse after excuse, that's not showing me respect, I think to myself. I remember I told her before we got official how important sex was to me to have a healthy relationship, so it's not like she didn't know, she didn't care. 20 minutes go by, "Next Friday it will happen" she says. Promise, I ask, she replies, yes.

I know you might change your mind, I say, she responds, no, I won't. I said, ok. Minutes after she leaves, I say, "Please start being upfront with me more," because this is now the fifth reason, she gave me why she didn't want to have sex. One week she feels ready and the next week she doesn't, so I'm confused.

The next day, Saturday, I look at my bank account, and my funds are low. We text through the day, and I say, I don't have the funds to see a movie and provide us both with transportation. However, I'm begging everyone I know for funds or a free ride for at least me, I also say, I know I wanted to hang out Christmas eve but because of low funds, I'm ok with waiting if you want. "Ok I'll come over, but it will be the last time for the next ten weeks, or my birthday, until valentine's day, deal?" she says, I reply yes, and even say I'd extend to 15 weeks.

Hours later, I don't want the deal if nothing will happen, please be upfront and let me know if you're rethinking it beforehand, it's going to hurt if you tell me at the last minute, I say, she doesn't say anything, and we talk the next day.

She texts me, "Still meeting." Yes, about 5 o'clock, if you're rethinking everything, please let me know. Hours later, they let me go early, my legs hurt, can you be ready at about 3 o'clock? Yes, she says, you haven't talked to me all day, should we cancel? Are we going to have a good night? I ask the only response I got from her was about 3:15, uber? It was on the way, I say.

The uber picks me up from work; I'm on the phone with my brother for most of the ride, I hang up and try talking to her, I get minimal responses. We pull up, and she runs up to her friend's door. We go to her friends for 45 minutes, as we walk down, she says, "You're on my shit list, for telling your coworkers about us." I tried not to for the past month and didn't; they know how broke I've been.

They'd even tease me about spending too much on her. However, I have a friend at work who's concerned. "I can't, I just recently started my job," she says. —she said that same reason five weeks before and said, "I just said that because it sounded good." We talk for a few then her friend's husband said, "she wants to see you."

As she goes back up, please hurry I yell as the uber is close. She doesn't return, and the husband of the friend comes down to let me know and attempts to give me her Christmas gift. At this point I'm feeling very hurt, teased, used, and played. I run-up to the door to see what the reason was then I call her twice, the second call she answers. Not meaning to, I yell through the phone, trying to express how hurt I am, and asking why you don't consider my feelings?

10 minutes later I got a text from her saying based upon my actions she's breaking up with me, and I wasn't trying hard enough in the relationship. I didn't mean to yell, but I was overcome with emotion. I text back "Please don't say that. I'm sorry." She wasn't accepting my apology.

A few days after we break up, I delete some photos off my phone and take our videos of YouTube Over the following days and weeks, I did a lot to try and prove that I was worthy of another chance. But she didn't care at all. I was in a four-month depression, friends told me to snap out of it, but I couldn't. I'd even be at work crying my eyes out.

I felt like my whole world came crashing down, my life didn't seem right without her, I'm crying all the time, I stopped eating, and I was awake for 60 hours in a row at one point. I loved her so much and still do, I was in shambles. I took Uber's to try and see her, I sent flowers, food, and stuff, and wrote to her sister many times on Facebook.

None of it worked, and I was foolish to think it would. The best thing to do after a breakup is doing nothing. In no way contact your ex, let them miss you. An ex will more likely take you back if you give them time and if they see that you are going about your life like the breakup isn't bothering you. I never went this far to try and get an ex back. Trying to get an ex back as I did is the wrong approach, and people tried to tell me. After the first two weeks of losing her, I didn't want to live anymore.

This girl is mean and very selfish, she only cares about herself. She will lie to make herself look good and like a victim. She said I never listened to her, well look at all the quotes I have in this chapter.

The quotes are what she said. Did she ever think "Maybe I'm confusing him?" No! selfish people don't think like that. If that did cross her mind, the outcome would have been different.

I poisoned myself and went to the hospital for two days. Then 2 weeks later. I started to read a book about breakups, and it helped a bit, I learned how to improve myself for when I start my next relationship.

Towards the end of March, I began to get over it slowly. One way I tried to get over it was writing a short book about it which is the title of this chapter. Do to me going overboard to try and get her back, she obtained an injunction on me.

On April 17th, 2018 we went to court. The judge said to her "Do you not see how much he cares?" No, she's selfish, the judge also expressed that we look like a good couple and he's sad that we couldn't work out. He did, however, sign a one-year injunction.

As I am writing this version on September 2, 2019, I have yet to be in another serious relationship since this one, although I have been looking. I do at times miss her but I know that she wasn't and never will be right for me. I have never fallen asleep and had dreams about an ex, but since the breakup she has appeared in a few of my dreams. However, I can honestly say I am over her and have very little feelings for her.

Chapter Six:

Moving On With A New Outlook

I went full time for a few months at work, it started in the middle of my last relationship. I liked working full time, but I couldn't afford to take care of my health by going to see a doctor.

So, to get Medicare back, I had to be on some social security check. I then soon found out that for the past 3 and a half years, before my SSI got cut, I should have been on SSD because I'm working.

In April I switched back to part-time at work, and in the middle of May, received a nice chunk of change from SSD.

In June I once again made a mistake of moving someone into my place. My friends know how alone I am and know that I want a relationship. So, this weakness was used against me to move someone into my place.

I was told to let her stay because she might be into me, which was far from true. Out of kindness, I allowed her to stay for free, thinking I'd benefit from it. I didn't, and my usage on my electric wasn't a concern to her, and she didn't respect my place. She was only here for a few months luckily.

On July 11th I left for the biggest vacation I ever took, which includes two cities. Los Angeles was the first; I arrived after departing from Tampa Florida, I had a layover in Atlanta.

I'm staying at the Anderson Estates like I did in 2017, it's a hostel in central LA, and close to a Metro Rail line. The nightly rate was $25. I liked staying here and it's in a good area. The staff here is very cool, and so is the owner, who's here Monday through Friday. The owner remembered me and said that I was always welcomed.

Within the first 20 minutes of arriving the staff offered to take me to the grocery store, Food for Less, it's like a Walmart for only groceries. After I put my food away, I went to Hollywood. I went to the Hard Rock and then Dave N Busters; they have happy hour 3:30-7 pm Monday-Friday and 10-close Monday-Thursday.

Thursday the 12th I started the day at 3 pm, by going to a tour at Paramount Pictures. The tour was from 4-6 pm; I got a t-shirt for $22 as a souvenir. I then took the Metro bus to Hollywood, in Hollywood they were offering a ride for 30 minutes in a Ferrari or Lamborghini to the Hollywood sign for $89, I took it. After the ride, I went to Dave N Busters I had a jack and coke for $3 and a snack.

Then I went to Hollywood Park Casino, where I spent only $70 on drinking and playing. The casino is tiny and only has table games, they are 24/7, but they do not serve alcohol after 1:30 am. When I returned to my hostel, I ordered Tommy's Hamburgers, they are only here in California and make chili burgers.

Friday the 13th I started the day at 3 pm and went on a tour, TMZ Celebrity Tour, it was from 4-6 pm, the route was from Hollywood Boulevard down Santa Monica Boulevard and then into Beverly Hills. After the tour, I ate at Dave N Busters because I prepaid when I booked my TMZ tour. I then went to a few bars on Hollywood Boulevard, the average price for a beer is $6. At one bar a PBR was $4.

Then I when to a bar called Jameson, a small picture of beer, which amounts to 3 beers is $7.50. the Jameson bar was one bar I really liked so; I went there quite a few times.

Saturday the 14th I went to Westfield Clover City mall, where I bought three outfits and shoes, I spent $185 there. Later that night I went back to Jameson bar until 2 am. Sunday the 15th all I did was go out at night. I took the Metro to Santa Monica, and then a bus to Venice.

I visited a bar called Cabo Cantina; I remembered the place from a year ago. It's a fun and friendly spot, the staff is very nice and so are the

158

regulars that go there. Every month they feature a beer, that beer is then $4 all month. Their happy hour is Mon-Fri 4-8 pm and Sun-Thurs 10:30 pm to 12:30 am, all drinks are 2 for 1.

Monday the 16th, a day of touring. Started at the California Science Center at 11 am. I went to In-n-out burger in Hollywood from 1:55 to 2:40 where it was wall to wall packed, I spent about $10.50 on lunch. I then toured the Dolby Theater, where the Oscar's are held, at 3. Then at 3:45 I toured the world-famous TLC Chinese Theater. At 5 I did a celebrity homes tour with Starline. From 4-4:45 I had a beer at Dave N Busters and paid $2.50.

Tuesday the 17th, I did a 2:30 pm tour at Sony Pictures, to get there I took the metro rail and two buses. Then biked on the beach between Santa Monica and Venice, spent $4.95 on coke on the beach. I stopped into Venice beach bar and grill, as I was walking from Santa Monica to Venice on Ocean Ave, I spent $10.50 on two beers. Then I got Mac-N-Cheese balls at a café for about $9. Then I stayed for a couple of hours at Cabo Cantina.

Wednesday the 18th from 2:30 to 7:30 I was at CBS studios. I was in the studio audience for The Four, a singing competition that airs on FOX. We sat there for 2 hours before taping began, the director tells us when to applaud and do other things. We sat through the first half of the show; then the audience was switched out. It takes about 2 hours to shoot the first 45 minutes of airtime. I then went to get wings at Hooters on Hollywood Blvd.; I spent about $22 for ten wings and a beer. After that, I went to Cabo Cantina.

Thursday the 19th I did a 2 pm tour at Warner Brothers Studio. I took the Metro rail to the corner of Hollywood and Highland, then Ubered from there to Warner Brothers. The tour was approximately 2 hours. Then at 5, I was at Universal Studios in Hollywood. Where I got a hotdog, chips, and a souvenir refillable drink for $20. I did the studio tour at Universal; it was an actual theme park ride; it was enjoyable and funny. After the tour, I went on the Transformers ride, which had technical difficulties right at the ending of the ride. I then went to Dave N Busters in Hollywood until 2 am.

Friday the 20th I stayed in a suite. I checked in about 1 pm, I met a girl on a dating app, I was looking for someone to chill nude with me in the hotel. She came about 4 and right away got naked. She asked if I wanted to have sex, I said "Ok, but wasn't looking for that, we did, and she left around 5:45. Then I left soon after. I went to dinner at the Hard Rock in Hollywood it was like $22. I then went back to my suite, by uber and took a power nap.

I then went to check out a strip club called Crazy Girls; I took uber there. I just wanted to see it because I saw it in one of my favorite shows, Entourage, I paid $20 to get in, and I stayed there for 20 minutes. I then spent the rest of the night at Jameson bar.

Saturday the 21st, I stayed at the Hostel all day. I made some friends, that evening I went out with them. I was going to a house party in the Hollywood hills. We were halfway there when the leader of our pact got a call; the police shut it down. We got out of the Uber in Hollywood, and a few minutes later got an Uber back to the Hostel. When we got back people were hanging out, one girl was extremely drunk, and she was passed out.

At around 1:30 am she slowly wakes up. She starts taking off all her clothes and falls in the pool. I think there's something wrong, but I'm the only one there. But she's ok and spends 45 minutes swimming. Sunday the 22nd I went to Cabo Cantina, took uber at 10 pm stayed there until 2 am.

Monday the 23rd, I flew from LAX to MIA with a layover in ATL. My plane got delayed after we pulled away from the gate in ATL, so I landed in Miami about 12:15 am (Tuesday). I then checked in at Miami Beach International Hostel, although I was tired from flying all day, I went to a bar after I got situated in my room.

I stayed there for four nights, the staff was friendly, and the Hostel was clean. Check-in didn't take long but however, I went to the wrong hostel at first. The bar I went to is a bar that I visit every time I'm in Miami Beach, Lost Weekend. This bar is the best bar in South Beach, it's cheap, clean, with friendly staff and guests. It's a bar you must visit. The bar draws a lot of tourist and locals.

Tuesday the 24th I started my day a 3 pm, I went to the nudist beach, I took the bus, and it was about a 45-minute ride up the beach. I like using bus S because that bus stop's the closest to the nude section of the beach. That night I went with my Hostel to Mangos Tropical Café, I made some friends buy going out. I paid $60 for the wrist ban to go that night and to go on Thursday on an island boat party. We got free drinks for one hour.

Wednesday the 25th I started my day at 11 am. I went to the nudist beach again until about 2:30. Then I went back to the hostel and ate dinner. That night I went with the friends I made the night before, bar hopping around Downtown Miami.

Thursday the 26th, I got up around 1, and we left for the boat party about 3:40. The boat party went from 4:15 to 7:30. The boat sailed from downtown and parked for 2 hours at an island. We had a Bar-B-Q with free beer, wine, and soda. Going on the boat party is fun, and well work the money.

When we got back, I paid $20 to go out that night with the hostel to STORY nightclub. The club was cool and fun. However, a beer is about $9. Friday the 27th I stayed in a hotel room and slept a lot. That night I went to Lost Weekend and watched a show. I stayed out until about 4 am. Saturday the 28th I checked into SoBe Hostel. One of my best friends came down from Boca to hang out; we did for an hour.

At 6:30 I ate dinner at the hostel and went to Lost

Weekend at about 9 that night.

On Sunday the 29th, I went to the nude beach

from like 3:30 to 7. Then that night from 11:30 to 5 am

I was at Lost Weekend. Monday the 30th, I moved up a

few blocks to another hostel called, The Hostel. I got to

check in about 12. after checking in, I decided to go to a

mall in South Miami, Dadeland Mall.

I just hung out there for 3 hours. From Miami

Beach I took a bus to the Government Center, then the

Metro Rail Green Line south. To go back to the beach, I

did the same thing just in reverse. That night I went

back to hang out at Lost weekend.

Tuesday the 31st I went to the Seminole Hard Rock in Hollywood, FL. From the beach I took the bus to Downtown Miami, then the Metro Rail north. Then I got the Tri-Rail to Hollywood. I was at the Casino from 3 to 8:30.

The main reason I went to the Casino was to meet up with co-workers, who came from the Casino I work at in Tampa, FL. After the Casino, I took an uber to Lost Weekend. Wednesday the 1st. I went to the nude beach for most of the day and then Lost Weekend later that night.

At the bar, I talked to a few girls like I always do. But tonight, I was in for a cool surprise, one of them

168

said: "Hey were you at Jameson bar in Hollywood, CA.?" I replied, yes. I was talking to her friend at the bar a week and a half ago.

Days after I returned home, I started creating a travel site, coreytravelguide.com, to educate low cost traveling. My website tells you how to take trips and where to go, without spending a lot of money.

Chapter seven

Life After First Publication

My first publication of Chapters Of Life was the last week in October 2018, but I had a lot to learn. I re-published about 7 times before I had everything correct and my real final draft was published by December 2018. Chapters of Life has 5 different versions. The different versions are font sizing and line spacing. I originally did this so I could differ the price. I started selling books in December at $10, the price has gone up since.

In November I had a breakdown out of the blue and got backer acted after trying to overdose. I took like 20 pills, I just got said about life. I stayed in the hospital for 4 days and was released a day before thanksgiving. As I was in the hospital, I was in class for my master's degree. After the holiday I called my school to drop my class, but I immediately retook it 2 weeks later.

As I am in school, currently working, and sell/promoting my book, I begin writing another book. I started writing a fictional short novel about traveling. This new book took me 5ish months to wright. Also, in January I started talking to and being friends with benefits with a new girl.

She told me she didn't want a relationship but liked talking to me and fooling around with me. Our friend with benefits relationship lasted about 6 weeks, because sometimes I called her on my way home from bars feeling depressed, she didn't like that. The last time I did that I almost got fired the following morning because I was 2-hours late for work.

After her and I stopped talking I stayed focused on me and doing my own thing. When I was not at work, I was out selling books. I went all around my area to shopping centers and bars selling books. In March I went back to my hometown of St. Petersburg for a weekend. I went to the mall and to the bars downtown, I had a good time back in my hometown.

Also, in March I announced my plan to move to LA in the summer. With that I booked a plane ticked and started paying for places. I also had a plan to go visit Miami one last time before moving to the west coast. Towards the end of April, I went to Miami for 5-days. Going to Miami this time was different because I am a writer and I took books to sell.

On Friday April 19TH I worked and after I got off, I headed straight for Miami. My best friend drove me from Tampa to Miami Beach. We left Tampa around 8 PM and I got to my hostel on South Beach around 1:25 AM. At about 2:25 I took Uber to Lost Weekend and stayed there until close. I sold 3 books in the bar. Saturday was my first day in Miami I got up around 10 and cough a trolley, it was the wrong one and took me way out the way. After riding for 40 minutes I got off at the front of Lincoln Rd. mall and walked like 4 blocks through the mall. Then when I was by the bus stop, I stopped and got food and beer. I then took the bus most of the way to the nude beach then ubered the last few miles.

I was at the nude beach from 2 to 7 pm, I sold 2 books and met a group of people. Later that night I went to my favorite bar, Lost Weekend. I was there for about 3 hours and sold 4 books, then when I realized I had 145 Just in cash I went to the casino. I had quite a bit to drank and played roulette, I won $180 then walked away, then after a while tried my luck again and I ended up winning $300.

On Sunday, I got up around 5 and walked around South Beach. I had no reason to sell books because I only had a few left and I'd just won $305 at the casino the night before. So, after arriving 48 hours ago in Miami with $455 I was sitting at $725. I went to a bar abort 7 and drank, then I bought myself my own hotel room for $139. it was on Ocean Drive. I went to the room from 8 to 9:15, then back to the hostel just because I bought a wrist ban to go out to the club with them. I hung out with the hostel clubbing for 2 hours, then took a cab to my favor-ate bar. It was around 3 when I returned to my room.

The next day, I got up around 11 and went to the nude beach. I was there form about 2:15 to 6:45. I then took the bus back down to South Beach and stopped for

175

food, on my way to the hostel I stopped at one of their sister ones and traded a book for a wrist band to go on that nights party. - I spent $75 this night

On Tuesday, I got up around 5PM got ready to go out. Before I left the Hostel, I met a girl at the bar downstairs, she bought my book and I sat with her and her friends outside. We chilled for about 45 minutes then I went out as they took a nap. I went to the sister hostel of mine, Rock Hostel and knew the guy at the counter form previous night's parties and previous years, he bought a book.

Then I went to their bar downstairs. I sat at the one stool left between a girl and a couple. I order a beer and ask the bartender to look at my book, I only had

two. then I say to both the couple and the girl "I wrote

this book." they both look at it and the girl immediately

started talking with me. As I sit there, she keeps

wanting for my attention, even if I'm looking at my

phone. we talk and talk and she's starting to put her arm

around me a lot. At 8 pm I ask what her plans were, she

said "Meeting with friends."

An hour later she's still sitting there with me, I

ask "Don't you need to go?" "No, and I don't care what

my friends think, your amazing and meeting you is

once in a lifetime, plus your way more interesting. her

phone has lots of messages from her friends, like,

"WTF" and she replies, "I met this sweet boy." After

sitting there for about an hour we go to Lost Weekend

and spend more time together. We dance and kiss a bit, she also nibbles my ear lobe, ran her fingers through my hair and beard by 1:30 am she gets herself a uber home, as she has to pack for a 6 AM flight. I go to Mango's and didn't get back to the hostel until 4:25.

On my last full day in Miami, I went to the nude beach from 1 to 6. made 3 new Facebook friends. On my way there I stopped for beer, water, and food. when I left a homeless couple, my age gave me a ride to the hostel. I could have taken the bus, but I wanted to help them, I gave them $15 for the ride than uber would of been, lol. On the way we get beer and drank. that night I went to lost weekend, my favorite bar in South Beach, I ate and drank a lot there.

The next day, I checked out of SoBe Hostel at 11, but stayed in the common area until 2:28. left to go to the airport but I stopped at Lincoln Rd. for a bite to eat. From there I took the bus to downtown and got the orange line to the airport. I got on Megabus at 4;25 and arrived home in Tampa. On the bus I met a cool businessman who was looking for a hotel, I helped him find one and we even went to one of my favorite bars in Brandon- total (not counting home) i spent $45 on this day.

After this trip I only about 6-weeks until my move. I started a class and it would be my last class before my scheduled leave of absence. In May I finished and published my second book- The Literary travel. I quickly began selling that along with my first book.

My move plans changed a little, instead of going directly from Tampa to LA, I'm going to make a 9-day pit stop in Miami. My reason was to try and meet up with that girl again and promote and sell my second book along with my first.

6 weeks before I moved, I met a girl online who was homeless. She stayed there with me and really liked me. We did "IT" quite a lot and she wanted to be in a relationship with me but couldn't because I was moving to follow my dream. She moved out 2 weeks

before I moved, and I got really focused on me. June 14th was my final workday at the casino, where I had worked for 7 years.

I left Tampa Bay, Fl. On June 24th and my best-friend drove me down to Miami. I stayed there for 9 days and sold about 35 books at $20 each. One night at a bar I met a girl and we did something in the bar's bathroom. On July 3rd I left Miami and flew to LA to start my new life.

In closing, it's September 7, 2019 and I'm living in LA now and just got a new job. I have been selling books on Hollywood Blvd, and my sales are good.

At the end of July, I lunched a children's book. I'm

planning to finish my master's degree in April of 2020

as well as another fictional short novel at that same

time. Chapters of Life, part 2 will be in a few years.

Money Saving Travel Tips

Q: What's a hostel and What's the average price?

In most cases a hotel style with a living area and rooms, some rooms have up to 12 beds. The more bed's lower you pay. In Los Angles, Threes a mansion as a hostel. I've <u>never</u> paid more than $25 a night, even in NYC for New Years.

- In Miami, at times the lowest hostel price is $14/night.
- In Miami, some provide FREE dinner daily.
- In Miami, hostels provide discount VIP club entrance.

The lowest price for a privet hotel room in Miami Beach is $69/night so, let's do a **one-week example.**

Person "A" is staying in a hostel that charges $17/night with free dinner, for one-week Person "A" is paying about $180.

Person "B" is staying in a hotel that charges $75/night , for one week Person "B" is pay about $525 + at least $12/day for dinner. In total Person "B" pay's $586 just for logging and dinner.

Person "B" is paying $400 more than person "A", only because he wants a privet room.

Q: **Public transportation**

An average 7-day unlimited travel, via bus/rail is no more than $30.00. Uber and Lyft are also options. In LA and NYC they have subways, subways and busses are no more than 20 minutes apart. There is not 24/7 service in all areas of LA, and no service for at least 3 hours, VIA bus, on Miami Beach.

If using a rideshare service such as Uber, consider using uber pool. Using pool lowers the cost of the ride because you are sharing the vehicle with other riders.

If you choose to dive your own car or rent a car, in some areas you will have the added expense of paying for parking. For example, in Miami beach you pay to park anywhere at any time. I believe it's $4/2-hours or $50/day.

Taking public transportation, meaning the bus or rail, is the best and cheapest option. Taking public transportation can save you at least $75 when getting around.

Flying?

Book smart, most round trips I've paid no more than $275.00, except for July 2018. Tuesday and Wednesdays are the cheapest days, and early morning/late night

Beer drinker?

Miami beach, LA, San Diego, and NYC, I've found beers as little as $2.50 to $4.00 per beer, at places and specific hours. So, shop around it's out there in any city

Made in the USA
Middletown, DE
27 September 2022

11244926R00113